THE WORK ANXIETY POEMS

ALAN CATLIN

ROADSIDE PRESS

THE WORK ANXIETY POEMS
Copyright ©Alan Catlin 2025
ISBN: 979-8-9996256-2-5
Library of Congress Control Number: 2025946862

Cover Art: Gene McCormick
Editor: Michele McDannold

Roadside Press
Meredosia, IL

Table of Contents

2-Anxiety

"Living with alcohol is living with death close by."
Marguerite Duras

The door will swing shut
When the door closes, no explanation is needed
I wish you would close it gently.
A Japanese Death Poem by Suzumi Suzuki

For V who makes everything possible.

1-Work

Insanity

They all end up in the bar eventually,
on foot, in wheelchairs, livery cabs,
stretch limos, riding mowers, wearing
torn-at-the-knees tuxedos, ties askew,
wine stained and bloodied or in track
suits after running a marathon chased
by demons, plain clothes cops, packs
of feral dogs only they can see, in bib
overalls so caked in manure they can
barely breathe or in hospital gowns
double knotted at the back, their life
savings in fanny packs around their
waists, blood type and date of admission
typewritten in plastic wristbands they
hadn't bothered to remove or in clown
suits, rugby shirts, laid-out-for-viewing
formal duds, punked out and glittered,
their eyes so glazed they can no longer
see, all of them laughing at jokes without
punch lines only they can hear, talking
to friends so far gone they are no longer
memories, ghost lights flickering from
their fingertips where they touch glass.

The Brood

They are the after-Christmas shoppers.
Decked out in their sartorial rags,
peering into the new check your luggage
lockers. Father adjusts his brand new
straw cowboy hat with the natty feather
on the side, testing the doors for heft,
moving down the line, one after the other,
puzzled by the locked ones he pulls
and pulls on without success, encouraged
by the brood, dressed to kill in kind,
scavenging the Mall, from the phone tills
to the trash baskets overflowing with
discarded, unwashed redeemable nickel
cans the Price Chopper will not accept.
While the young ones work over
the newspaper vending machines,
next, they scavenge deserted lots,
occupied houses backyards or anything
portable that can be removed.
Mother tries to explain to all who will
listen, the awful truth that the end
is near and it may well be once Security
gets word that The Brood is back in town.

Blocks God Forgot Just Off Western and State

Every city has one, a block God
forgot, some unofficial war zone,
demilitarized, but alive and active
with all the usual suspects cops roust
on periodic missions to clean up after
some particularly rowdy disturbance,
something so embarrassing, around
election day, even the mayor is moved
to act. After the votes have been counted,
results confirmed, the war goes on as before.
911 calls come in and cars are dispatched,
later rather than sooner, except, in cases
of extreme cruelty, events that make
front page news or, on occasion CNN;
'Fraternity hazing involved terrorist
techniques, pledges for unchartered
frat subjected to punishments, not unlike
water boarding, until they were forced
to beg for mercy.'
The cries from basement/ dungeon so loud,
so horrific, even cowed neighbors
could no longer endure the noise, could
only imagine what must be happening inside.
University officials assert they had
'suspicions banned fraternity was still
accepting new members,' as they had been,
banding and disbanding time and time
again, for fifty years, only the names
and faces changed; the philosophy and
personality types the same.

Over the years, the block has been modified,
buildings burned out, abandoned,
strafed in territorial feuds, boarded up
or razed, salt sprinkled on the mounds left
behind, for sale signs riddled with bullet
holes, gang graffiti ornamented, relics
no one cares to recall or revisit.
All the former denizens, drug dealers,
and their whores moved on, occupying
new digs that soon resemble the old:
from Odell to Kelton, from Elberon to
Quail to Washington; forsaken places,
reclamation projects so far past due
only those with no future go there.

Pictures at an Exhibition

Detective Sgt. wants a
positive ID on one of these
women.
"We know they've
been hooking out of here
weekends, you had to see them,
shit, whores are big tippers,
especially on weekend tricks.
Why are you stonewalling us?
We know they've been greasing you,
hell, a blow job's gotta be
worth $20, what's a blow job
in the Men's to a bitch like this?
Come clean and we'll drop
the whole shitload.
All we want is a positive make."   '
None of them looked familiar.
I felt totally stupid, completely
out of it, a loser going nowhere
on a Monday night. I almost felt
like taping their mug shots to
the back bar mirrors and playing
love songs on the juke until one
of their faces started to make sense.
I ID'd one with blonde hair
and a tattoo of Pegasus rising
between her breasts. Detective Sgt.
seemed satisfied with the make
even if we both knew it was
a lame lie.

Somehow, closing at 4AM, downing
boilermakers against the big chill,
I could almost see her getting pretty,
combing her hair out, applying
fresh lipstick in the back bar mirror.

Good Friday

Maybe he was just another cruel
joke by God on the world left over
from a bad experiment involving
full moons, hallucinogens and an
alcohol psychoses. Laughing at
inner jokes made him a stand up
comedian performing live in a
Twilight Zone of his own creation.
Expounding from his personal size
Book of Paul was Show and Tell
time for the Happy Hour audience
of the impenitent. Confiscating his
beer, draws a reaction he equates
with the wrath of God:
"What's your problem?"
"I'm tired of watching your version
of Laugh-In, it was old years ago."
"I'm not finished with that beer."
"If you want it, you're going to
have to swim down a drainpipe to
Menands. It's a long haul and it
smells like hell down there."
"You're messing with God."
"I don't think God has ever been
to Menands, I'm sure he wouldn't
like it much, Menands is the
antithesis of the Garden of Eden."
"I know the Angel of Death, personal,
you're doomed, now. I'll see you dead."
"Try squinting out of the other eye

for a change, maybe you'll get lucky
and catch me in a frozen frame.
Let's try a new subject now, like watching
you leave."
"I'm Jesse James, I'll come back and
rob you."
"That's okay, my name's Bob Ford,
if you're up on history, you'll back
out that door."
He was fairly well read for a psychotic,
knowing what that meant, usually they
just throw things and get taken away
to the Psychiatric Center for a fun
weekend of observation.

They came from the school

that held certain truths to be
self-evident such as:
IF YOU CAN'T FUCK IT
BLOW IT UP. Truth and
beauty, succinctly contained
by one short sentence,
broken up into fragments
and reprinted on both sides
of formerly white t-shirts
they had worn through
the pub crawl of death
that began early Friday
morning on St Patrick's
Day, and seemed about
to end here, at some vague
time after midnight on
the Sunday after, all hell
broken loose and running
rampant, in the smoking
wasteland behind their
eyes, somehow plastered
wide open by some evil
combination of Irish whisky,
draft beers, and high-test speed.
The concept of having had
too much, not sticking
to the few remaining
sentient cells, despite
all the barman's best
efforts to deny service,

still, they persist, waving
filthy rumpled five
dollar bills high over
their heads as if they
were leftover pennants
from The Ancient Order
of the Hibernians Parade,
muttering gibberish,
back benchers at a misplaced,
endless Irish Wake.

A Counting Fool

There was no
obvious reason
for what he was
doing other than
he was a counting
fool, flipping pages
as rapidly as he can,
toting up the score
of some game only
he knew who was
playing, what the
rules, stood leaning
on a near empty
shelf at the end
of a Non-Fiction
aisle of the down-
town public library
roughly a third of
the way through
a non-circulating
reference copy of
what could have
been an encyclopedia,
volume unknown
and a long way to
go, so many paragraphs,
to tabulate, so little time

In the Cinco de Mayo dream

I'm epically drunk. Not happy
drunk or tipsy drunks but *Under
the Volcano* drunk. Beyond ossified
though somehow, upright, mobile,
weaving through Day of the Dead
trinkets laid out on display on
the ground for sale, or use, later on
for spirit walks up narrow, hard,
dried lava path to the dormant,
blackened pit, where the fire gods
once shot burning embers into soot
darkened sky like a cosmic fireworks
display.

I'm hot. Infernally hot and coated
with the sweat of something that
was never human. Even asleep,
I feel lightheaded, disoriented,
befuddled and confused looking
for something to drink amid rubble
of fenced in front yard. Amid discarded
trash and cerveza bottles in a garden
of dead and dying things one bottle
has a huge, fat, distended worm
engorged with what only could be
vital fluids of some form of animal
life. Nearby the bottle there is a bucket
of blood with an Alice in Wonderland
sign that says DRINK ME. And I do.

Hear Us Oh Lord from Heaven Thy Dwelling Place

is the hymn quoted on their
mass-printed pamphlets that
collect in every gutter, half
frozen puddles, and garbage
receptacles all around town,
a fact of life that leaves them
undeterred in their mission
to spread the word of a savage god,
who unleashes them in all
manner of unholy weather
the young, old, and infirm alike,
all touched by some kind of
kinetic force that makes
their features glow in darkest
night, a St Elmo's fire speaking;
bright on the outside, a vacuum
inside.

The Light That Failed

Even in the dull dark of the barroom,
minutes before last call, his body inert
as seaside rock after a punishing
storm. I could see flickers of light
like Coleman Hurricane lamps in each
hooded eye, a rank odor of sweat,
stale beer, damp clothes & kerosene,
the scent he exuded, as he tried to translate
the concept of cocktail into speech,
the blackened ends of his fingernails
drumming the lacquered bar top for service,
an unearthly sound emanating from between
split lips suggested he was landlocked now,
a lost spirit now an ancient mariner
in search of a wedding to attend.

The Breeder

They had to have been let loose
from The Projects, some kind of
government assisted, low-rent
dead-end hovel wasteland for
professional single-parent Welfare cases

Her oldest daughter clearly retarded,
one deformed foot pointing the wrong
way, crossed eyes uncorrected,
barely focused on supermarket produce
she lunges for to fondle and to molest

Unclean siblings scattering in all directions,
grabbing unattainables: plastic toys,
animal play-things, magazines, newspapers,
anything not too heavy to lift or secured
behind locked doors

All returning to the mother, screaming of
how they want—, how they need—, how
they must—

Failing to obtain, they are suddenly afflicted,
desperate for restroom facilities on the other end
of the store, one at a time pleading they can no
longer wait, can no longer retain

Pleas the mother ignores, pushing her baby
cart with two squeaky wheels, hiding who-
knows-what under the sleeping, oversized brain

dead one inert inside, stuff everywhere except
where it matters most; on her supersized-for-
maximum-use/expansion body, see-through
filthy white tank top, too small stained and torn
shorts splitting at the seams, worn through at
the crotch, no underwear beneath

No one stops her when she grabs the nearest
junk food, possible pacifier, 100% sugar coated
non-food and begins handing out the contents
to the brood; open mouthed cashiers praying
for a lightning strike, an alien invasion, anything
that will prevent her from choosing their line.

The Chronicle of Young Satan

was going to be the title
of the bestselling book
of how he ended up as a mass
murderer of unspeakable violence.
He had that special, strange glow,
the truly weird have, a kind of
gauze covering his eyes that
filtered out any traces of
humanity threatening to leak in.
He even smelled strange like some
kind of mutant life form, undecided
what shape to assume next.
In between shots of Tequila,
he whistled through the gaps where
front teeth should be, formulating
the question of the afternoon,
"I haven't eaten in days and I
need something solid in my
stomach. Got anything with
a worm at the bottom of a bottle?"

War Prayer

Everyone in his platoon had been
killed or maimed in Tet, or, maybe,
it was at Danang in 68 or 69,
it wasn't clear which, but, one thing
was certain, what had happened to him
was as immediate as yesterday, and
always would be, and no amount of
Stout with Power's backers, was
about to change that, nor would
the Special Forces prayer he was
mumbling to himself, before he downed
each shot, and slid the dead soldier
across the bar for a refill, losing
track of the body count, consuming
the evidence, an internal atrocity
no statistic could ever account for.

To a Person Sitting in Darkness

sitting at the far end of the bar
after hours, the silent TV,
flash dancing MTV images in the cold,
harsh, early dawn lighting.
What is left of the bar's interior,
covered in spilt beers, rank whiskeys,
smoked cigarettes; all the filled up
ashtrays of post-midnight dreams.
Five pints of Bass Ale, and two double
extra dry Robert Roys for the road,
doesn't touch, or remove the darkness
lingering inside. The only motivation
to move, a force of nature,
an empty glass.

Election Day Results in the Village of the Damned

"I'll bet you're glad
Election Day is over.
It was like the Village
of the Damned in here.
There were lots of bodies
around but all of them
had eyes that were
propped open staring ahead
at nothing. Really eerie.
The last time, I saw
eyes like that was a buck
spooked out of the woods
on a starless night.
It was the same thing
down below, a lot of unhappy
campers working the wrong
end of a ten percent
solution to life. That was one
wait staff that looked like
they were getting ready to
turn in their tip trays
and look for a regular real
job. Somehow, I could tell
you knew exactly how they felt."

Lab Rats

"That smart mouth Assemblyman
from the City could hardly wait
to finish touring the Lab
facilities to ask The Question:
'Where are they keeping all
those drug addicted rats I've been
hearing so much about?'
It was all I could do to refrain
from pointing out that they were
living in all those subway stations
he took to work back home but an
image of him actually waiting for
a subway wouldn't materialize.
Not that it mattered, if you read
some of the statistics we've been
handed recently most of
the human race is a lab rat now.
He should have been here twelve years
ago to investigate the gold fish
bowl thing where they were feeding
goldfish Chivas. There was a hue
and cry over that one!
No one could really question
the findings, who really knew about
the tolerance factor of fish anyway?
There was a full-blown report, though.
Mostly, they were pissed off that
the lab boys were feeding them Chivas,
why not rack stuff for Christ sake?
Much cheaper and that's the bottom

line these days make no mistake about it.
I had to give the boys credit, though,
I could see them toasting the fish:
this shot's for you and this one's for
me, down the hatch, boys.
Ingenuity is a strong suit in our
department anyway. We're not called
the Department of Drug and Alcohol Abuse
for nothing."

Day Job

Setting up for the banquet,
he's a hurting bird, unable
to bend over for anything.
"What's the matter, dude?
You're too young to be that old
and crippled."
"It's my day job. I don't know
if it's me or what but they seem
to be sending us all the porkers.
That last babe must have tipped
the scales at close to 400 lbs."
"Things are tough all over."
"That's not the half of it,
as soon as it gets cold,
they're coming in two or three
at a time, one larger than the next.
It's about time to can my day job."
"What the hell do you do?"
"I'm in the Death business,
I work for my old man's funeral home.
It'll take years off your life:
if the smell of flowers doesn't get you
the preservatives and disinfectants will.
Besides, who wants to tell your kids
you carry stiffs for a living?"

Just Like Something on TV

We were watching the fire on
the 12 o'clock News two people
would end up dead in.
"Better there than in Albany.
You know how many people I've
put in rubber bags? After a while,
you don't care anymore.
You can't or else it gets to you.
The first time I saw one, we were
hosing down a tough one and
we're getting the live ones out
and isn't there this thoroughly
drenched, pissed off old lady,
yelling like a banshee at us to
turn off the water because we
were getting her all wet.
I thought she was going to hit
one of us with a frying pan or
something, I honestly don't know
how she survived, the place was like
fully involved. Later, they found
a dead old guy in a backroom.
Captain said to me, 'I want you
to check out that room. There's
a dead man in there. Look careful
and if you have to be sick or feel
like crying go right ahead, no one
cares, we've all been there before.'
I felt real odd checking the old
guy out, it was almost as if he wasn't

dead or even real somehow,
no big deal, I thought, just like
something on TV, until later,
I couldn't hold a beer steady I was
shaking so bad. That's when I knew
how real it was."

A Tramp Abroad

She was one of those girls
that was born of age,
a virgin converted at birth,
conceived to inspire an exotic
sexual fantasy that could never
be fulfilled.
It wasn't difficult imagining men
dying for a couple of weeks as
the object of her desires, or,
even torments, just as long as
the potential for having her,
even as an afterthought,
or as an object of contempt,
remained a possibility.
I thought she was capable of much
bigger venues than this one,
working some outback lounge
in a medium sized city Upstate,
instead of the strip in Vegas,
or along the halls and backrooms
of Broadway.
She had what every talent scout
in the world was looking for in
spades, and she wasn't afraid to use it.
Maybe she was looking for a new agent,
or just slumming on her own.
Whatever it was I didn't mind.
Lit her cigarette when she was
ready, slipped her one or two on the House,
as pathetic as the rest of mankind,
indulging an impossible dream.

The Third Policeman

on the scene sd.,
" You don't usually get
to see that kind of mess
with only one victim involved,
outside of a crime lab
workshop on blood splatter
distributions caused by
various kinds of blunt
instruments on the human
body.
The perp must have
thought his Big League
tryout depended on the success
of his stroke, points of contact,
and power hitting technique,
the way he worked that
sucker over.
One thing for sure, when we
nail his ass to the wall,
downtown, he'll know all
about major league hitting."

The Hard Life

began for him long before
birth: his insides mutated,
all those genes his mother
used as a kind of
perverse free-form
genetics experiment,
that began in the tail end
of the 60's and hasn't ended yet.
You could sense his conception
as a riot of bad unprotected sex,
cheap booze, and more
pharmaceuticals than a well-
stocked, on-campus infirmary.
Nothing he ever did or said
made sense, nor had he ever
achieved anything like focus or
anything like an interpersonal
relationship, most ending
before they began.
His mother claimed he hardly
ever cried as a baby once she
started him on Similac and
homemade acid.
She could tell he was grooving
on the stars, the way his eyes rolled
behind the lids and his extremities
twitched just like he was dancing.

Three Weapons of the AntiChrist

"I was working the jail in Troy
the night they brought in this Jesus
freak for interrupting a Service.
I never knew it before but there's
a law on the books makes that an
arrestable offense.
First, I guess you have to imagine
this fried out on who knows what
kind of drugs, long-haired, unwashed
maniac interrupting your sermon
to tell you about The One True God,
as distinguished from the one you've
been telling all these misguided people
about and, then, everything starts
to make sense.
Needless to say, he wasn't about
to let a little thing like getting
arrested and having his ass hauled off
to jail dampen his missionary zeal,
not with all these designer drugs
in him along with the mood.
In fact, he's making so much noise
he's got the whole compound upset.
Finally, the Sergeant in charge had
enough, grabbed a pair of cuffs,
a roll of duct tape and a nightstick
and says, 'I'll take care of this
one, pronto.'
Sergeant gets down by the Jesus dude's
cell, holds up the cuffs and says,

'Yes sir, I see. Those are to bind
my hands together so that I can't make
the signs of the cross.'
'Good for you. Do you know what this is for?'
'Yes sir, I do. That tape is to seal
my mouth so that I can't say the names
of the One and Only True God.'
'Very good. Now what do you think this is for?'
'I have no idea, sir.'
'It's to open up a six-inch gash in your
head if you don't shut the fuck up.'
We didn't hear another word out of him
the rest of the night."

Burn Baby Burn

I had a $7000 suit once.
I was living with Fatal
Attraction out in the mansion.
Everything was honky dory
in the morning when D-
picks me up for work.
You know, the usual, kissy
face, huggy bod, have a nice
day. Little did I know she
was having a major love
affair with an Absolut bottle
and a bag full of Xanax.
While she's settling in to
watch this movie on HBO
or, maybe, it was The Romance
Channel, with her you never
know. Anyway, this bitch in
the flick gets even with her
man for, God knows what,
probably for breathing too much
air or something horrible like
that, probably he has no clue
what he did, but she knew, that's
for sure, and that's all that matters.
So, the movie bitch takes all
the dudes clothes, stuffs his car
full of them and blows the sucker up.
Kaboom: Burn Baby Burn—
Reminds me, did I ever tell you
the one about what the difference

between a bitch and a slut was?
A slut sleeps with everyone &
a bitch won't sleep with you.
Well, my woman was one of
those rare slut bitches. Enough
to confuse any man. So, I get
home from work, say, Hey dear,
that's some fire you got going
there. how many logs did you
throw on anyway? I looked a
little closer. That's when I started
getting a real bad feeling, like,
what were all these metal buttons
& shit doing in there? Remember
that nice leather coat I had?
Went the way of the $7000 suit.
Boy, was she ever gone by then.
I could tell 'cause her head was
bobbin' around like one of them
slinky toys. One thing I learned
that day, the line in the joke
should be, a bitch burns all
your best clothes and then wants
to sleep with you next to a
roaring fire. All I know for sure
is that I'll never live in a house
again, that has a working fireplace.

What was left

of his poor mouth she
was trying to hold together
with bar towels, torn cotton
shirt sleeves & handkerchiefs.
If she'd seen him bite
the edge off of that pilsner
& start chewing just before
that from-the-hip sucker
punch connected,
she might not have bothered
no matter how much
she thought she loved him,
might have realized what
everyone else had known
for years, he had it coming.

She had "To Have"

tattooed above her
right breast, and,
"To Have Not" above
her left one.
Wore a low cut,
Harley Honey t-shirt
with no bra beneath.
Had a phoenix rising
between the two tattoos
and was rolling her tongue
between the gap of her
front teeth as she asked
for, "Jack Neat
I like my stuff hard,
what about you?"
I was more of a
wet and wild man
myself and said so.
"Maybe I'm just
the woman you're
looking for."
"Maybe I said."
playing along,
wondering what
that was all going
to mean, if anything.

She used a circus

clown name like
PNIN that made
me wonder where
she had done
her basic training
in the acrobatics
of love. It must
have been one
hell of a trade
school the way
the bar flies
flocked to her
side and whoever
had laid down
the cash for
her schooling
didn't have to
travel far or look
hard to see
it was money
well spent

I was supposed

to be impressed
that he was the star
of some movie
with a bogus title
like The Real Life
of Sebastian Knight
as opposed to the fake
life or something
like all the monogrammed
paraphernalia he wore
from the production
as if he were an
apprentice Al Pacino
Searching for Richard,
a movie made mostly
in parking lots
& public parks
buildings with permission
in Saratoga Springs
& Bennington, a film that
never made it out
of the can at Sundance
& maybe had been shown
to paying audiences twice
or three times in Small
Arts Festivals Theaters
in big cities on either
coast & had just about
covered costs of about 10k
I heard him complaining

to his evil twin who looked
like a fey version of
Dorian Gray, "I Just hate
being in the provinces.
You can hardly ever get good
bottled water." as if that was
why you came to a bar
with 21 beer taps
& 28 flavors of bottled beers
in the first place

Happy Days

They drank rounds
of Stout that never seemed
to end, baby Powers,
"Ah, for the love
of God I love all
my babies, all of God's
lovely blessed little ones."
Each shot cradled
almost solemnly
each pint lifted
a reverent act
fresh glasses touched
honors a new beloved
one sanctified
What they were
doing memorialized
the dead and what
lay beyond, while
at home, his real
little ones starved.

Company

His company was a light
infantry platoon,
an irregular army
of dropouts and misfit
drifters like something
out of a Classified
Advertisement in
Soldier of Fortune
magazine.
You could hire them to do
just about anything
and not one incriminating
mark left behind,
sort of a permanent
garbage removal service
where no waste product
was too noxious or
intractable to handle.
One thing for sure,
wherever they had
been was never the same
after, like they were
some kind of permanent
war waiting to happen.

Every bachelor

party starts out
heading on some
out-of-control
cruise mission,
a blind rush up against
a wall, motherfucker,
more pricks than
kicks, getting tossed
out of bars, loud
and rude beyond belief,
excess hormones
determining exactly
what the body did,
without benefit
of the brain,
All too often this
last hurrah, this last
night on the town,
ended up being ticketed
on the toes, zipped
into body bags as
the latest fashion
in formal wear.

Those Who Fall

He waits his turn,
hot for love, too impatient
to sit in the front room,
wound tight as his
shirt collar. Noises
from her bedroom are
coiled springs letting
go inside him.
Outside, on the walkout
porch, the air is so cool,
fresh as a woman's
breath on his neck
and hair. Porch railing
for leaning back on,
support, for slugging down
the last of that half pint
of dark Barbados Rum.
That is, unless the railing
is not secured, as the one
he puts his weight on,
falling from Grace,
as that was the name
she called herself as a,
kind of joke, or so she
would say, later, after
the three point landing
of her john-to-be,
on the front steps
of her walkup, that night,
long ago, on Steuben Street.

Albany's Finest

Sure, we pulled
down on this guy
and wasted him.
I don't care what
color he is, a guy
half-naked, screaming
like a psycho:
Death To All Pigs,
charging officers
with BBQ fork
and knife with
an arrest record
as long as Elberon
Place doesn't
stand too much of
a chance against
a loaded, drawn
service revolver.
I mean, what were
we supposed to do,
check his ID?
Everyone knew who
he was already.

Brownie

I used to
have a wife
She left
me A kid
too, maybe
I fought in
the war
That's what
messed me
up Drugs
never man
but I liked
to drink
so much
lost my job
lost everything
I haven't
eaten in
two weeks
Look at me
You think
I like
living on
the street
    ?

They called him "The Paratrooper"

at Shooters, a no-
parachute-needed
daredevil diver
from obscene heights
like the crawlspace
between drop ceiling
and upstairs bar floor,
into the Ladies,
too blind drunk
to see from afar
or near, for that
matter, somehow
evading capture
despite the flooding
caused by his direct
hit landing on a
commode and subsequent
deluge, evading
that is, until his
eventful, unwitting
return to the scene
of his crime for
a nightcap that will
be spoken of as legends
are in bars for years
to come.

It was developing into

a Do the Right Thing
bus ride, despite the
temperature at twenty
below with the wind
chill. The brothers
in the back of the bus
were in an evil mood,
cracked out and freezing
for forty minutes waiting
for the running late bus
from hell. No amount
of rap sheet music can
soothe this kind of
savage beast. All this
bus needed was the dude
who got on at The Mall:
"Where you going?"
the bus driver demands.
"What the fuck do you
care, I ain't paying no
fare no how."
"Well, this bus isn't
going anywhere until you
do."
"The hell it isn't. I got
me some heavy shit says
it is."
"I've got all night, I'm
so late already, I don't
care anymore."

Which was a major bullshit
line for the brothers,
getting psyched with evil
vibes from the Walkman
pounding in their heads,
the cold of the night
about to be splintered
by spinning red lights,
riot guns off safety.
It might as well end here,
their eyes said, come and
get us, we got nothing left
to lose

Home Brew

He was one of those
guys who spent most
of his waking life in
bars that served Old
Milwaukee out of Bud
taps and no one ever
knew the difference.
Listening to his dark
thoughts on the hidden
nature of man and beasts
being nothing more than
empty shells some sick
creature put on earth
to piss on whenever
the mood was upon him,
made me think his idea
of an imported beer
was probably Schlitz.
"It's imported alright.
It's from Milwaukee."
Somehow it wasn't
difficult to imagine
his wife draining three
quarters of his Coors Light
bottles and burying them
neck up in the garden
for the slugs to refill
and in good time replacing
the caps to mix them in
at random with the ones
already chilling in
the fridge.

Black Is Black

was tattooed on his right
forearm, Los Bravos on
his left as he drinks Alabama
Slammer shots in rapid
succession, pounding the drained
glass on the bar with
increasingly louder and more
annoying percussive statements,
the red, clinging fluid
coating the rim below
the black painted line
of each shot glass staining
as blood stains, filling
the soaked sponge of his
overflowing brain leaking
from his nose, his swelling
tongue, his eye sockets as he stands,
vaguely aware of a shape behind
the bar saying, "Para Los
Olvidados, No?" and touching
shot glasses with him one
last time before the darkness
settles in for good

Working Girl

Small sips are all
she can manage
from brown bagged
Tall Boy beer, too tired
to move from this spot
in the sun, her eyes
permanently bagged,
clothes wrinkled, dirty
hair uncombed,
a mess, as always,
burned out beyond
belief, well into
her middle age, in
her twenties, yet
somehow, ageless,
this sad eyed lady,
on leave from fucking
the endless armies
of the night.

Long after last calls

after death by high speed
car chase down crowded
city streets, long after lights
run, after stop signs blown,
after bumper car hits,
after fire hydrants blasted
off, even bystanders sing
the blues. See the men in
blue with guns drawn,
EMT lights spinning,
knowing nothing can be done
for the minding-his-own
business-guy on the receiving
end of the head on crash;
after taking a hit like that,
after the jaws of life applied
there is nothing left to save.

After wills and testaments,
death certificates signed,
the rebuilt woodie in the garage,
Johnny Walker Blue bottles
dust settled, uncorked, shot
glasses forever turned down,
Cognac snifters unused,
Amontillado aging badly in wine
rack, Fuisse going off as well.

After the quadrophonic sound
system remains dormant,

long playing records on turntable
spindle, unable to drop, wilted
flowers browned and brittle
in cut glass vases, cold hearth
and potbellied stove ash piled
and fallow, the only sound
the ice maker in the freezer
dropping bell shaped cubes
into the void.

2-Anxiety

May Day Dream Poem

We're in a place that feels
like Japan. I assume we are in
Tokyo because of the congestion,
the neon, the sensation of being
with millions.

I'm with an Albany Poet,
Dan Wilcox, and we're in
a car trying to find our way
to the baseball stadium.
I sense we may already be late
for the opening ceremony
which we don't want to
miss.

We're in a kind of Uber vehicle
and our guides are two Russians
who look disturbingly familiar.
Like Lev and Igor from the Mueller
Report fiasco and they are clearly
jerking us around. We manage to lose
Igor, as Lev seems to know where
we are going. It seems to take
forever to get there, in slow motion,
but we do.

My wife is already at the game
and she has scored a cool, in English,
replica of a team jersey with the number
of one of the players we loved,

from another era, on it though it isn't
clear which team it is or what player
the number represents.

I'm obsessed with finding a Suzuki
jersey but they don't have any in my
size. The sense now is, the only reason
we have come to Japan is to score
souvenirs. A feeling of abject despair
is overwhelming.

Dan has done the sensible thing,
found our seats, and is sitting down
to watch the game. I am hitting up
all the vendors on this futile quest
for souvenirs that don't exist.

I'm not sure which teams are playing
or who to root for. I used to be a Giants
fan but I heard from a friend who knows
about these things, that the Swallows
are better.

It gets dark early and there are no
lights. I realize the game is over
but I don't know who won.

I am alone in Japan looking for a
Russian Uber driver that knows our
language, a real spirit guide. I don't
think he exists either. I'm beginning
to doubt I'll ever find a way home.

Work Anxiety Dream

Even though I am sleeping,
I dream I am awake, that
the term paper is due in a week,
finals as well, all of Byron to
read, Shelley, three novels,
learn German overnight for
competency test for the degree...
Fear of failure is worse than
the failure itself, working all
night in part time job going full
time, reading until my eyesight
begins to fail, fear of going blind,
like Milton, we also serve who only
stand and wait. Working, behind
the bar, watching the rathskeller door
open and close, open, and close, no one
entering or leaving, everyone in
the library asleep or about to be,
all the drinks being served are on
the house, now I'll be fired or fail
for sure, but I can't determine which
is more real or which is worse.

Ex Post Facto Work Anxiety Dream

I wasn't supposed to
have these dreams after
I retired but there I am,
at the bus stop, waiting
for the one that says,
"Express Albany"
but no buses come.
I'm already late and
beyond stressed about it.
It's St. Patrick's Day,
the busiest bar day of
the year and people are
counting on me to be on time
plus, it's a huge pay day despite
all the bullshit you have to
put up with to get it.
Maybe because of all
the bullshit. And when
the bus comes it says,
"Albany" but the driver
says, "We're taking a little
detour." And I ask, "Where?"
And he says, "To the end of
the of the earth." Which is
Troy but I don't know that yet
and a dude in a Jesus Gets Us
tank top says, "I'm okay
with that. I feel good about
where I'm going." But I don't,
remembering the first time

I worked Kiss Me I'm Irish
and there were two fights an hour
until midnight and then it got
crazy but I think maybe that was
a different work anxiety dream.
Or was it? I can't tell the difference
any more so I ask the driver
to let me off anywhere, don't
care where and he does but
I don't know where I am,
I might be anywhere, I might be
nowhere, so I take the first bus
that comes along and I ask
the driver where we're headed
and he says, "Nowhere."
Which sounds just about right
and a dude in a Jesus Is Love
tank top asks me if I want
a copy of the good book?
And I think it's going
to be a long night, a good book
will help pass the time,
so, I say, "Sure, why not?"
But when I see what this good book
is I regret my choice. Just my luck.
I'd already read it and it wasn't
that great.

Another Saturday Night in Jukebox Hell

I am surrounded by a haze
of smoke in a silent space
that used to be the pre-renovation
tavern bar trying to hear what
the old guy is ordering.
Whatever he is saying sounds
like a whispered foreign tongue
I can't make any sense of and
I wonder where all the other
people went? What happened to
the noise that feels like a living
thing you have to ignore even
though it influences everything
you do, Not that I miss it but
it feels so odd not to be able
to hear in that space left behind
by the absence of noise with only
a smirking much younger woman
standing nearby until I finally shout,
"Speak up or forever hold your
peace. "And he says,
"I want an orgasm and a pint."
I think about replying, "A pint
Of what?" but, instead, I say,
"That's a White Russian with
Amaretto to you, son."
So, I make the drinks and then
it's late, very late. The bar lights
are down all the way, a damp
musty haze, distinctive to bars,

clings to everything, even me,
and this young, well-dressed
guy wants red wine. Lots of it.
And, I say, "No, you don't.
What we serve is swill. Worse
than swill. Even the winos won't
touch it." But he says, "Pour away
and open up another bottle."
"But it's corked."
"All the better."
"And this one will be corked too.
I can guarantee it."
"Great. I don't care. My date
and I are celebrating. She wants
red wine, come hell or high
water, and she'll have it."
"This ought to cover everything."
He throws a few portraits of my
my favorite dead president,
Ulysses S. Grant, on the wood.
"Whatever is left over is yours."
Which would be a couple of hundred
bucks, less a dollar ninety-eight
for the wine and I think,
whatever is the key word here.
So, I open the bottle. Pocket
the green, it's St Patrick's Day
after all, and wonder why it's
so quiet. Where is everyone?
Maybe it's the day the music
died as well, and no one told me.
Then the jukebox turns itself on.

Loud. Selects The Kinks,
"You've really got me.
You've really got me.
Girl..." And then the smirking
girl is back at the bar with her glass
asking for another orgasm.
"You know how to make those, right?"
And I ask, "What happened to
your old man?"
"I got rid of him."
And I wonder if she means, like
Permanently, but I don't say anything.
"I can make you a Screaming Orgasm.
All you have to do is add something Irish."
"Are you Irish?"
"I can be if you want me to be."
"Go for it." she says.
As I make the drink, I wonder if this
is last call? Or had someone called
for the end of time and I missed it.
Was where we were well past that now?

Work Anxiety In the Lake District

First orders come from
above through murder holes
drilled into the floor where
the main bar sinks overflow
and the slop sinks leak.
The waitress is sleeping,
head down on the invisible
cellar bar while a rush of
patrons arrive, walking single
file down misaligned stairs,
chanting verses from a Pink Floyd
song, shouting out orders as they
pass into the well-lighted, unfinished
basement lounge. Second orders
come over the bar from everywhere
at once but all the bottles are
somewhere else, up flights of stairs
others are using, all the taps open
and free flowing but the glassware
is inaccessible in too tall, overhead
racks, in too low cabinets you have to
lie down next to in order to retrieve
what lies within, reaching hands
scraped and bleeding on rough hewn
wooden shelves, on the chipped and
broken glass, still more orders come
and there is no room to move,
the basement ceiling pressing down,
more murder holes being drilled,
delivering last orders from above.

New Job: a work anxiety poem

I am, fashionably late for my
new job at the restaurant I was
heavily recruited for. Tim,
the day guy from my last job,
is working the stick, and I say,
"Just like old times." And he says,
"Yeah, but not really." And I wonder
what he means. As if he is reading my
mind, he says, "You'll find out."
"Where's your tie?" Is the last thing
he says before he disappears and
I notice I'm not wearing one
from my famous collection of hundreds
of ugly ties. And that I forgot to change
from my way-too-short grey cotton Champion
brand of workout shorts,
though I did remember a freshly pressed
long sleeve shirt that went out of style
around 1969. Also, I have on my navy
blue, no sleeve, pullover sweater vest
so, maybe I'm okay. Maybe no one
will notice I'm only wearing shorts.
The customers only see you from
the waist up, right?

I'm dismayed that the long bar I expected
is only four stools that look like something
left over from Romper Room and that the speed rack
is chest high. Not only that, it has all
the wrong bottles in it and all of them are plastic,

which really sucks, and they have pre-measured shots
Not a speed pourer anywhere; all of this impossible
to work with. Not only that, the so-called lounge,
has only a couple of Salvation Army reject
vinyl covered sofas with sawed off legs
and a busted in the middle coffee table
to rest drinks on.

The whole place looks more like a luncheonette
than a cocktail lounge, but I'm here to work so
I ask the waitress where I get my Guest Checks.
She says, maybe I should I try the other restaurant
a few doors further down the mall and I think,
"It's come to this, mall work. I swore this would
never happen to me."

Instead of following her suggestion, I look around
the place until I find a book and I'm about
to tear a page off and go to work when I notice all
the checks are filled out. I say, "Someone
is going to be really pissed at me.
Someone named Sandra." And she says,
"That's me and I haven't got time to be pissed off."
Smiling as she says so intimating that she likes me
and that hanging around might be worth my while.

Instead, I walk to the other end of the bar,
into another part of the mall, in search of a place
I might be able to buy a tie. There doesn't seem
to be any clothing stores but I do meet a well-dressed
dweeb who wants to know where the bartending job is.
I point toward the place I just came from.

Boy, is he in for as surprise, I think.
I'm pretty sure he won't get the job.

Morgan in half-light: a work anxiety poem

Morgan out of focus, blurry at the bar,
talking, as he would, despite
having nothing to say. His left
hand cradling the right where
the Merit Light burns like
a perpetual flame with budding
ash. Where a half-empty, lost its head,
pint of Budweiser sits on the wood ,
where he leans talking, nearing
that stage of drunkenness where
the confessions will begin:

How he hates The Church and
all priests, despite most of his
crew's work is in stained glass.
Remains bitter having
to pay bribes to have his first
marriage annulled and how the second
wife is so cold to him, as if
someone should find solace with
a man who is drunk every night.
How his personal doctor told
him that his blood pressure is
beyond through the roof and that
if he didn't quit drinking, he might
pay the ultimate price. How he
switched to red wine because he
heard it was better for your health,
starting each morning with a few
tumblers of grape juice, as he calls

his new libation, with his corn flakes,
not that he actually eats cereal.
The vision is so immediate, so real,
it is almost like he was still alive,
as if the strokes never happened,
the lung cancer didn't kick in,
go dormant and come back with a
vengeance, almost as if he wasn't
confined to a wheelchair in a long
term care facility instead of living on
his own with enabler who used up
men on the edge as if they were
toys to be played with then destroyed
and abandoned for newer, fresher
toys. It was almost like he had never
earned the nicknames of Fixture
for being always present like the furniture
that the place seemed incomplete without
him. As if his other nickname wasn't
moron for stuff he said even the red
neck loud mouths thought were extreme.
It was almost as if he wasn't so much
a memory as a restless spirit that
refused to die, almost a revenant
reaching out, asking for another beer.

Flickers: a work anxiety poem

The first image is a snapshot
of a memory he never had,
that he made up for us to
see him as a special forces
airborne ranger in the jungle
on a mission he was too young
to have volunteered for but
claimed to have been on.
The image he must have seen
in a book like *Requiem* of pictures
taken by photo journalists killed
in South East Asia of a solider
with OB's face holding a string
of human ears with a shit eating,
proud as hell, grin.

Then it is the image of himself
as a Troy cop in a uniform he never
wore, diving into the Hudson
after a car submerged and sinking;
a woman inside you couldn't save,
clawing at the driver's side window.

Then it was him dressed as a nurse
at Memorial where he claimed
he was a graveyard shift working ER
and oncology though the head of nursing
told me she never heard of him, and
there he sits, telling us how awful
the cancer patients were as he lights
another cigarette.

All these fantastic still life images
flashing by like a science fiction
movie of photos only progressing
in time but never moving in
themselves as if he were a kind of
Zelig, everywhere and nowhere at once.
more like a patient in One Flew Over
the Cuckoo's Nest than an orderly.

Then he is strapped in a kind of seat
upside down and unable to move
like a character in Cronenberg's Crash,
then like a kind of Jaba the Hut hooked
up to a hundred intravenous tubes in
a Naked Lunch...

All these images flashing faster and faster
finally freezing on the one from the last
time he was at the bar looking like a
pale, enormous, crew-cut Shrek, claiming
he was a medic now in The National Guard
in Massachusetts and they were probably
going to ship him over to Iraq....

And no one offered to buy him a drink,
for the road though they all wished
he would just go, anywhere not here.
Me most of all.

Five Years After: a work anxiety dream

Even on the five-year anniversary
of no longer working the bar job,
the nightmares of being there as
real and as immediate as being there
ever was, feeling bound, frustrated,
blocked, hindered in every way imaginable,
making the hard work, impossible,
the easy work just as bad, but the demands
to do the work never cease, everyone
wanting something, the walls closing in
on all sides and the boss man the most
insistent of all, as he erects new obstacles,
until I feel as if I am standing before the law
in an Orson Welles movie or, as K, the accused,
committer of non-existent crimes and already
convicted, the death sentence to be executed
just before dawn, or, worse, never, and the work
goes on and on and on.

Bleeding: a work anxiety dream

Finally dozing after being unable
to sleep. Anxiety dreams, immediate and intense.
No longer do they focus on undergrad
academic failure, flunking out, the unknowable end.
The end in those college days meant
a place like Vietnam. Oddly, no anxiety
dreams of grad school, though the workload
was twice as bad, no sleep then, between
classes, assignments, working a late night
job. No sleep, then, for years; living on
beer, empty gas tank fumes and beer.

The anxious dream centers on the work-
place, introduces a wound, a glass cut
to the bone, blood in the ice. No one
cares. It's all about the bleeding self
carrying on, working, tending bar
one handed for ten hours without a break.

Everyone who sees the wound says
it needs stitches. Lots of stitches.
The bleeding wouldn't stop, the stained bar rag
slipping, hanging loose around the wrist.
But there I am, building cocktails with my right hand,
deliberate, but carrying on, all fluidity lost
for the duration. No one cares how I feel,
if the wound is dealt with or not.
No one cares how I am unless the drinks
are tainted.

Abu Ghraib: a work anxiety dream

That one where you are
transported to one of those
torture chamber prisons in Iraq
where they apply hoods with
no eye slits and strap you into
stress positions and play
repetitive bass line music/noise
punctuated by a kind of bell so that
you feel as if you are only half-
conscious/passing out and a voice
accompanies the noise chanting
in a foreign language you think of
as Urban, not one recognizable as
an actual tongue but something
like one, endlessly repeating spat out
hate infused syllables so you plead,
"I'll talk. I'll tell you anything."
But they don't want you to talk.
They want you to suffer.

A Work Anxiety Dream with Lydia Davis in it.

I'm back in the tavern again
and its wall-to-wall humans
though it could be worse as previous
night terrors have shown.
Everyone is smoking clove cigarettes
to cover the smell of hashish hookahs
emanating from the blind corner
to the left of the bar that I can't see
in my back bar mirrors.
We're all in the midnight witching
hour, stuck in jukebox hell, listening to
The Best of Patsy Cline,

" Worry, why do I let myself worry?
Wondering what in the world did I do?"

Then the new general manager is
behind the bar introducing herself as
Lydia Davis and I'm thinking what
the hell is she doing here? She doesn't
even look like the 70's version of Lydia
despite not knowing her then, I've seen
photos of what she looked like.

And she assures me she is the same
Lydia Davis so I just go with it and try
to find out when she changed jobs
and why but she's not interested in
anything I have to say. "Read this."
She says and turns to walk away and

I say, "Watch your step." But she still
isn't listening so I'm not surprised
when she steps in the place where the wooden
slats we walk on are broken, turns her ankle
and would have fallen flat on her face
if I didn't catch her.
"I knew you were trouble from word one."
She says, pretending
she can walk on a broken ankle.
"You'll pay for this." Lydia says.
And I say, "You can't fire me. No one else
can run this place."
" Watch me." She says.

And Patsy is crooning,
"Dreams I know can't come true
Why can't I forget the past"

And I wait for Patsy's plane to crash.
Planes have crashed here before
as I saw first-hand outside the tavern.
Patsy may be gone and I may be fired
but I'll be back. That's why they call
it jukebox hell.

Re-education Camp: a work anxiety poem

We've been sent to the Elon
Musk re-education camp to
reconsider our life choices and
to reorder our priorities.
I feel as if I should be resisting,
and they must as well, forcing
them to strip me naked and
shove me into a Whirlpool
sized basin filled with churning,
discolored, cold water. My two
attendants look like standard
issue strong arm enforcer types
left over from a black and white
gangster movie and they are grilling
me about Latin tenses, declensions
I never learned and try to tell them
my wife was the Classics major
but that only makes them angrier
and I sense they are going to
subject me to a water torture worse
than the cold water one involving
dunking, restraints, and prodding
with blunt objects, the kind of stuff
that used to be thought of as
therapeutic in asylums back in
the dark ages a few decades ago.
They don't have to be specific but
the implication is there will be blood
in the water before long and a noise
torture involving a Bob Dylan

imitator singing folk songs in Romanian.
Regardless of what happens next
my refusal to talk suggests I will be
blamed for everything that will go
wrong like when a private rocket
launch explodes and they will need
someone to pick up all the pieces
including the body parts. Like it or
not, custodial work is my future,
is my job now.

The Public Reading: a work anxiety poem

I'm sitting back stage waiting
for a number to see where I am
in the order of service among
the poetry readers having their
five minutes at the mic.
I told the organizers that I preferred
an early slot as the earlier I read,
the less my anxiety. Once, when
I was a late addition to the program,
words froze in my throat and I began
to stammer and it was almost impossible
to articulate, an agony that finally
ended when I managed an explosive
scream; "I Can't Fucking Breathe."
My slam scores were abysmal and
the judges voted me off the stage
and out of the venue. Another time,
I couldn't utter a single word, stood
motionless as if in suspended animation
or cryonically frozen. Let me tell you,
standing in front of a microphone
before a hostile crowd of open mic poets
staring up at you as if trying to turn you
into a pillar of salt is unnerving.
I felt like a Kafka character in search
of a story that has no end. What is
most troubling is, I know this is the most
important reading, I will ever give.
That my fate will be determined one way
or the other like a fallen gladiator awaiting

the emperor's thumb. Despite the organizers
telling me to prepare myself, that my
turn is coming soon; I am not reassured.
Even when they say, "You're next."
I can't move. I know my name will never
be called.

Night Walking: a work anxiety poem

All the addresses on
the buildings are the same

All the front doors
All the curtained windows
All the store fronts
exactly the same

All geometric as pieces
of jigsawed puzzle

a lab testing rat maze
you feel as if
you are walking in
but somehow remain
rooted in place

as the walls slide by
as the storefronts
curtained windows
front doors the same
of all the buildings
with the same address
on streets without lights
you cannot move on

out of breath
wheezing
from all the efforts
of standing still

all the effort expended
going nowhere

War of the Worlds Work Anxiety Dream

I'm working the bar in this
long World War 1 trench
on the edge of no man's land
tracer rounds overhead
like Wilfred Own fireworks.
All the soldiers, drinkers huddled
on floorboards sinking into the mud,
the slime, the shit.
All of them mumbling Latin phrases
Nos Moritus de Salutemus
as if the words might be understood
as a new form of cocktail death.
The further along the trench I walk,
the deeper it goes like ever expanding
gladiatorial passageways into a Coliseum
of no return arena.
In the stands, the spectators, are all
holding their thumbs down and wild
beasts are having their way with the slain
or the soon to be.
All along the deeper rungs are teller's
windows selling win, place and show
tickets for an underground ferry ride
to hell.
Although the lines are long, I'm eager
to join the queue, don't mind that
the teller at my window is blind,
accepts coin of the realm but gives
nothing in return.
All of us are waiting for the command

to move on when a whistle sounds
and the actor playing Kirk Douglas
goes over the top, waving for all of us
to follow him to certain death.
Before I can climb the ladder
with no rungs to higher ground a poison
mustard gas cloud descends and my
defective mask is leaking laughing gas
for all to breath.
That's when a new wave of soldiers
arrives bearing army scrip instead of cash
demanding everything under the sun
and I want to say we only take cold cash
but we are so far beyond rules and
regulations that nothing I could possibly
say could matter. Even when I run out
of booze I am tasked to make drinks
in an endless loop of no supply and endless demand.

Sleeper Awake: a work anxiety dream

I wake up in my dream though
I know I am still asleep.
I'm late for work even though
this isn't time for my shift.
They must have called me in to open
the day after a night I closed.
This used to happen quite often
at The Rib when Linda was working
as she didn't know where the bottles
went. So I'm getting dressed and
it begins to feel like the Dali dream
sequence in "Spellbound" inside
the bar I have been transported to.
And then it is raining while I'm rushing
to the bus stop and my umbrella is
full of holes but I'm moving backward
instead of forward and I'm going to be
really late and wet which also used
to happen all the time at The Rib
as traffic was so bad I could never
cross Route 5 . But I'm not working
at The Rib anymore, even in the dream,
it's The Tavern and one of the college
kids is already setting the place up,
so what did they need me for?
And he's taking rolls of quarters,
like a hundred of them from some guy
off the street and giving him all
our big bills and the owner's daughter
is cashing checks, so there is no cash

money at all in the drawer, just change,
more change than you could use in
a month but break a twenty? Forget it.
And the college guy is looking at me
like it's all my fault and like, what good
was I anyway? I'm like way too old to be
working in a bar. So I perform a couple
of drink making, sleight-of-hand tricks
and he's like Spellbound and I'm back
in that dream again, though it seems more
and more like that black and white flick,
"Kafka" and then the Welles noir, "The Trial,"
and I finally realize the only reason that I'm
there at all is someone has to get shot in the end.

The Bus: a work anxiety dream

Down the center aisle
they come, banging their
cymbals and their tambourines,
carrying terra cotta figurines
in their arms as if they were
sacred objects or balanced on
their heads as they march
past the seated ones, engrossed
in their papers, ears encased
by headphones in self-containing
worlds, oblivious to the blur
of scenery beyond rain streaked
windows, these center aisle
revelers becoming solemn as
mourners on a day of the dead
carrying lighted candles, exuding
a strange kind of electric light,
black smoke, in no air conditioning
bus, an oak coffin balanced on
broad shoulders of the bereaved
whose interlocking arms form a
monkey's puzzle in a garden of
unearthly delights, the driver
refusing to slow down to match
the mood, to unload at requested
stops, running all the lights,
oblivious to what is happening
behind all these fogged in windows,
with all these people trapped inside.

St. Patrick's Day as Hell: a work anxiety dream

After the early A.M. arrivals, the three-day bingers,
        eyes like pin holes in a black canvas;
After the heart attack machine, flushed face turning
        blue, a bite of corned beef on rye still
        lodged in his throat;
After the ambulances go, the police cars, Black Maria
        wagons,
After an Irish cheer for the band, empty pint glasses
        thrown against a wall and the shot glasses
        that followed;
After the banshee wail, impromptu a cappella singer,
        her wild red hair aflame with the light from
        a No Exit sign,
After the penny whistles, rogue bag pipes, fiddlers
        on speed and homemade acid;
After the relentless crush of revelers, the fetid air inside,
        thick as smoke following a terror bomb raid;
After hours in the bar, the blood draining morning toward
        dawn, rounds of Irish and Stout for the help,
        the Oblivion Ha Ha beckoning, Yeats with a
        magic flute gesturing to follow him this way
        into the dark.

Work Anxiety Poem: Hotter Than Hell

The lights are all the way up
in the back room in this dreamed
memory of the bar. Any light at all
back there is unusual, to say the least,
as it's always so dark back there
you need a guide dog to find
the fire escapes when you need them.
Luckily all the emergency doors are open,
letting in the heat and humidity though what we
need is cross ventilation and a breeze.

What's most disconcerting is I feel
I should check on the room that hasn't
been built yet and the patio outside of
that, which isn't there, because it's so
hot, stifling in fact, which is normal
as the AC unit is big and loud and makes
so much noise you can't think
straight but doesn't generate anything
useful like cool air. I seem to be arguing
with some random girl about turning on
the machine but I can't hear her over
the for-show AC unit and she keeps
yelling, "Turn it up, UP, it's hotter
than hell in here."
And I'm yelling back, "Don't you think
I know that? I'm wearing a sweater and
a tie and a formerly white shirt."
All of them so sweat soaked, it looks
as if I took half a shower with my clothes on.

Then I'm in the front room,
behind the bar, hemmed in by the noise,
the crowd, and what passes for music
on the jukebox. Being this crowded
is weird because all the people are
college kids who are gone for the summer,
even the ones who flunked classes because
they spent all their spare time here
instead of studying.

Odder still, all these kids
are from the freshman class of twenty or
so years ago, before the drinking age change
and they all are ordering L.I.T's, as they
are calling Long Island Iced Teas in those
days, but no one wants to pay, even though
they cost like two bucks fifty.

I'm working by myself, as usual,
so, when a bunch of guys try to bolt,
I have to block the door which isn't going
to end well as there are a whole lot
more of them than there is me.
Then I notice Peter the graveyard shift
cop drinking drafts and he's asking me if
I want them dead? And I say,
"I'll think about it."
Peter says, "Don't take too long,
I haven't got all night."
So, I don't.

Work Anxiety Dream: Stalker

After hours, lights down in the bar,
chair legs facing up on the tables,
only the EXIT lights glowing,
the click of the sound turned down jukebox
playing songs no one can hear,
random compressors kicking on,
shutting off, the ice machine dumping
a new load of cubes on the mounds
in the deep freeze…

Down the worn thin, unevenly spaced
stairs, into the low ceiling cellar where
the walk-in coolers full of beer are,
the leaking pipes, frayed electrical
wires, the single too-low wattage bulbs
on pull chains are and the wooden, sagging
shelves packed with bar supplies,
used guest checks, register tapes and
the overwhelming smell of sewage,
the creeping damp from the cobblestone
floor, the standing water the sump pumps
can't contain, where the footsteps not
your own follow yours in a hard-to-focus
gloom, each deep breath feeling like
the next to last one, as we move from one
shadow place to the next, opening long
forgotten doors into closets, new found
rooms that lead to other worlds, darker
places where the walls sweat and the all
in black man behind me raises his arm

holding the long wide bladed knife
as if to strike as another door opens
and a new phase of this hide and seek game
for keeps, begins.

Work Anxiety Dream: The Haunting

All the bar walls feel hot and achingly
alive. Even the windows are breathing,
in and out, bending as if they have been
made elastic to accommodate an impossible
move. I look into the back bar mirrors
and two of the three faces of Eve look
back at me mocking my uncertainty,
my fear that cannot accommodate
of the already low ceiling, with its fake
tin overlay, is shrinking, compressing,
inching downward into what feels like
a torture chambered night. Then all 12 of
the for-sports TV's turn themselves onto
different horror show channels, creating
a kind of cacophonous haunting in a dozen
different tongues, each more foreign
than the next that feels like a festival
of technicolor blood and gore only a real
human sacrifice can allay. All freezing
in place, soundless as an autoplay
on the juke cranks out the Iron Maiden
album, The Prisoner, "I'm not
a number, I'm a free man!"
Then AC/DC Hell's Bells, then Blue
Oyster Cult, Don't Fear the Reaper
but I do.

Half-Tone Beckett in Bar Light: A Work Anxiety Poem

They went down to the cellar
with flashlights and returned,
filthy, bedraggled as hounds
left in the rain to wallow in
offal and mud.
They decamped, mid-bar on stools,
that scraped the foot scuffed floors
amid the remains of a night of
serious drinking.
Seen from afar, well above the bar,
light is refracted through green
bar bottle glass like shards of
misspent lives, dissembled as
hobo Hoover towns like hoarse
voiced village criers delivering
messages no one wants to hear
around camp fires in 50 gallon
drums.
All the garbage of their lives
amount to nothing more than
left-behind stogie stumps and
cigarette end prophecies that mean
nothing in harsh pre-dawn haze
waiting for what the new day brings.

A Beast in the Jungle: A Work Anxiety Poem

Waking up after sleeping in
the heat, bar interiors have been
transformed into taxidermy dreams
that make no sense.
Bewildered, I feel like Captain Willard
in a Saigon hotel seeing the overhead
fans as chopper blades descending
into a jungle instead of safely, behind
the lines, where dreams are the enemy
and there is no escaping the prison he is in.
Instead of in country, I'm in the bar,
looking over Norman Bates' shoulder
at birds of prey poised to attack,
at pointed antlers from long dead
steers, hear the rutting elks in the zoo,
fear the mounted wild cat heads,
the rare white buffalo skins and
the signs that say: CAUTION:
DO NOT TOUCH ENDANGERED
SPECIES, as if somehow, touching
them might make them more dead
than they already are.
I can barely see what must have been
the bar beyond the walls of mounted
heads receding into the darkness with
each tentative step I take.
The darker it becomes, the louder the dead
animal noises become and the jungle
I was now in, more confining and alive.
I check my sidearm to make sure it
is still loaded and walked on.
What else could I do?

The Grim Sweeper After: a work anxiety poem
for Gary of the Floors r.i.p.

last call, lights up, lights down,
then bum's rush out, up again;
the grim sweeper works on in miasmic
fug of incipient dawn. Bar day's end
the bar is an assemblage of all that can be
broken, discarded, gutted: the chump change
and occasional huge pay day of cash wad,
lost wallets, ladies' handbags, members only
clothes, underwear: the bras, panties, boxers
and the briefs. All the blood and guts of party
going is his, all that lays at the base of
a fractured rainbow, the sweeper collects
in piles with a push broom, swipes away
with string mops and covers with wax.
All that puddles is removed, dumped
in drain sinks that clog after dumping
and still he sweeps, he mops, he collects
what is left behind; all those human remains.

Dormitory Fire: a work anxiety poem

I can smell the smoke from a dormitory fire,
in a building that would be attached to
the second floor of the tavern where
the overflow auxiliary bar would be if we
had one.
Though it is a semester break, there are a
few kids who have no homes staying in rooms
where fire alarms would be if the smoke
and the dorms were real.
My bar back rescues what could be
saved before the blaze becomes fully
involved.
I feel justified not helping out as someone
has to stay behind to mind the store.
Still, I feel a sense of guilt though
the authorities all say, "Just as well
you didn't get involved, the old guys
always get in the way."
Somewhat mollified, I am confronted
by a young woman from a 40 years ago
poetry workshop insisting she is my betrothed
though we both know I am married
to someone else.
The last time I saw her, decades ago,
she had short black hair cut in a page boy
but now it is dyed purple, shaved on
one side and long on the other with
curly bangs. "I just had it done," she says,
"how do you like it?"
I think it looks awful but I don't say anything.

Then she wants me to take her home and
do what must be done.
Whatever that might be.
We leave together but I don't know
where we are going.
Apparently, I have no say in the matter.
"Boy, are you in for a surprise." She says,
as if that was a good thing.
I know this is the time to object
but I don't say anything.
There is no explanation for any of this.

Day's End: a work anxiety poem

Locked inside, bar light down
as always, at day's end, sound off
on the wide screen TV above
the bar access point, channels change
of their own free will from music videos,
to concert performance art as Mummer's
Play, to a stop action Passion Play
complete with biblical verses
with subtitles in a language that hasn't
been translated yet, to a looking backward
from where I am now to yesterday,
then rapidly accelerating backwards
like an unedited review of my past life,
that I am powerless to turn off.
Then all the tv's, all twelve of them,
in all the interlocking bar rooms,
turn themselves on all showing the same,
increasingly blurry outtakes of my life,
stuff long forgotten and buried now vivid
and real like a terrible dream that won't end
until all the wide screens go blank and
a white noise replaces the images as the key
sensory input as if nothing had happened,
as if I were never there.

Work Anxiety Dream: No Exits

The sense is that my former
employer has a No Compete
option on my professional
services but as I have been retired
for over ten years, it seems unlikely
it could be applied. Still, I feel
guilty considering the new guy's
offer to manage as, "the obvious
choice," of a new bar in the cellar
where my first fulltime work was.
I'm inclined to say no but
this project is intriguing.
They show me around the place
which takes about two minutes,
as there isn't anything to see:
just a freshly painted square space
with no tables, chairs, stools or
even a functional bar. They say,
"You just have to imagine those
being there." I'm thinking this
project has more to do with *Room*
than The Tavern but I reserve judgment
until I hear their pitch. "We figure
that we can get maybe 200 or so
bodies in here." And I'm remembering
that the tavern in this space had
a max capacity of 120 and it was
wider than this one, as these new guys
seem to have figured out a way to shrink
the walls and raise the ceiling

while removing all the personal touches
that make a college bar a desirable
hang out." What do you think?"
They ask, and all I can think of is
the fire inspectors who used to hang out
here after checking out the high rise
mausoleums at the state school that
were being used as dorms saying,
"Those buildings are fire traps but this one
is worse. Where are the fire exits?
There aren't any anyone could get to,
are there?" I looked around, though
I knew they were right. I said to the new guys,
"200 bodies seems just about right."

Royal Shakespeare Company: a work anxiety dream

What I remember most about
the bar I worked in, hung in,
drank in, was the low ceiling.
The way the smoke clung to
the permanently water-stained,
nicotine discolored, abused
scuffed wood. The way sound
seemed to press down from above.
How the room always felt like
an implosion waiting to happen,
once the wall-to-wall humanity
squeezed in until you felt like
a character in an EA Poe story
that didn't end well.

Now, the room seems to have
expanded without changing shape.
Where the side bar stools used to
be, high back chairs are and a large
stage area extends from the door all
the way to the back room, an elaborate
wooden edifice like the one the RSC
used for Copperfield large enough to
accommodate a cast of thousands all
of whom are trying to speak at once
over the deafening sound of amplified-
to-the-max juke box noise.
Their costumes seem like something out
of a Monster's Ball and they all seem to
be shouting their demands at the man behind

the bar where I am trying to find the key
to the door that will allow me to ascend
a spiral staircase to my room on the fourth
floor but the key won't turn, the door
will not budge, so I am forced to try
the emergency exit stairs that are cluttered
with priceless family heirlooms,
then the scene shifts from Dickens to
Martin McDonagh's *Beauty Queen*
of Leenane, a set I thought was ludicrous,
whose characters were preposterous, until
I wandered into a random pub in Dover
for a Plowman's Lunch and there all
those people were acting out their own
variations on a theme by McDonagh.
I thought about the hover craft skimming
the waves, crossing the channel in those
days, long ago, before the warped hands
on the bar clock began sticking at quarter
to the hour and quarter past but still kept
time, time that I was running out of,
pressed as I was against the low and shrinking
ceiling, looking for the escape hatch,
the door that will not open no matter
how hard I push, no matter which key I try.

Snowbound: A Work Anxiety Dream

Maybe it was the wind in that dream
of being snowbound in the bar,
one of those dreams so real,
it's impossible after, to remember
what was real and what was dream
as I stand watching the snow drift
on Western Avenue, no cars moving,
no people walking, no cross country
skiers, nothing but the wind and
the still leafy tree limbs snapping,
falling taking the power wires with them,
no light anywhere but half a block
where the bar is, house lights dimmed,
MTV on mute Eurythmics surreality,
"Sweet Dreams Are Made of These,"
though there is nothing sweet
about this dream once the black
curtain is drawn down across
the bar and a spot light haloes
a silent talking head like something
out of Cassavetes and we're in
their living room improv acting,
uncomfortable closeups and heat
lamps inducing sweating fever dream
soliloquies then the light switches off
and we hear three voices like something
from a Beckett play set in a graveyard
with beer taps and Irish whiskey added,
and their voices modulate in a kind of
crazy loop tape summary of their lives

together, tales of love, and hate and
lust that death does not have the power
to end and then the ghost light behind
the bar switches off and there is nothing
but darkness, a black shroud that used
to be a curtain and the muted voices
of all the people who died here calling
for a drink.

Publication Notes

Many thanks to all the editors who chose my work way back when and not so long ago. And to Michele and all the Roadside gang for supporting my work.

Blue Collar; First Class; Heeltap; Disturb the Universe; Kind of a Hurricane; Beatnik Cowboy; Mama Yama; Dead Snakes; Snakeskin; Children, Churches, and Daddies; Unwound; Crimson Leer; Chiron Review; Inbetweenhangovers; Screed; South Ash; The Underground; Caffe Lena Anthology; Synchronized Chaos; New Verse News; Art Mag; Main Street Rag; Glimpse.

Alan Catlin worked for the better part of 34 years in his unchosen profession as a barman in and around the greater Albany, NY area. He has published dozens of chapbooks and full-length books focusing on his work and the people he met while laboring in the trenches of bar warfare.

More Roadside Press titles by Alan Catlin:
Bar Guide for the Seriously Deranged
Another Saturday Night in Jukebox Hell

MORE ROADSIDE PRESS TITLES

MORE ROADSIDE PRESS TITLES

Licorice Heart
Miles Budimir

Disposable Darlings
Todd Cirillo

Full Moon Midnight
Belinda Subraman

Innocent Postcards
John Pietaro

Cistern Latitudes
James Duncan

*Another Saturday Night
in Jukebox Hell*
Alan Catlin

Abandoned By All Things
Karl Koweski

Ain't These Sorrows Sweet?
Lauren Scharhag

*Gregory Corso:
Ten Times a Poet*
Edited by Leon Horton

*She Throws Herself Forward
to Stop the Fall*
Dave Newman

*We Don't Get to
Write the Ending*
Aleathia Drehmer

*These Many Cold
Winters of the Heart*
Ryan Quinn Flanagan

*Things You Never
Knew Existed*
Josh Olsen

Maze
Jennifer Juneau

Green Roses Bloom for Icarus
Hiromi Yoshida

Let the Scaffolds Fall
Shaun Rouser

Apocalypsing
Jason Anderson

Failing to Fall
James Griffin

Last Bacchanale
George Wallace

Thrift Store Jackets
Karl Koweski

Night Bird Flying
Danny Shot

*All Skate: True Stories
from Middle Life*
Lori Jakiela

*Cloud Watching
in the Inferno*
Westley Heine

Current Disasters
Jen McConnell

MORE ROADSIDE PRESS TITLES

Better Than The
Best American Poetry
Dave Newman

Perseverance:
The Making of a Musician
Steven Grey

Little Graveyards
Aleathia Drehmer

Fatherless Children
Michael D. Grover

The Screw City Poems
Richard Vargas

A Better Loser
Nathan Graziano

and all of us drinking the blood
of our enemies
John Sweet

The People Are Like
Wolves to Me
William Taylor Jr.

This Is Where We Are
Nicholas Claro

Collected Poems (2005-2025)
Michele McDannold

With Her Hair on Fire
Christy Prahl